All about INFIDELITY:

How to Heal and save your Relationship

By

Karen P. Ellis

Neither in part nor full can the document be copied, scanned, faxed or retained without approval from the publisher or creator.

TABLE OF CONTENT

INTRODUCTION

You or your spouse must have cheated. You can now decide to split up or stay together. If you opt for the latter, you should begin the often-stated but usually extremely challenging task of rebuilding the trust that the sexual stray shattered. If you've ever been the victim of infidelity, you undoubtedly listened to your lover when they said that you can still make things work if you just repair the trust. But is this ever really possible? Can you mend the trust that was broken? there isn't a straightforward answer to this issue. However, this is not to say that after an affair, a couple cannot rebuild trust. The conclusion is that the answer is "yes," but it won't be easy. Any effort to regain trust will be made by someone who is committed to maintaining or regaining the pre-cheating condition of affairs. People who aren't emotionally invested may decide to give up and leave. When someone's trust is betrayed, they experience the same level of emotional grief as any previous time they have experienced betrayal in the past. For someone who has been through what they've been cheated on to assess the betrayal they are currently feeling in isolation while still carrying around the emotional baggage from previous heartache brought on by cheating. Only you understand the particulars of your bond, your feelings, and whether you can once again rely on this person completely. But if you do decide to work on things, how do you go about restoring trust?

CHAPTER ONE

TALKING TO YOUR PARTNER

GET READY FOR HIS ACTION

The majority of cheating spouses will deny cheating until they are blue in the face, so be ready for that.

Even if you show some of them the proof, some of them will still deny having an affair. Songs have been written on this, proving how accurate it is.

WHY?

Because you are "catching" him off guard, even if you believed that he was your greatest friend and the only person who would never lie to you in this way.

He doesn't yet have his tale together, and he isn't sure if he wants to admit cheating, How to inform you of it,

How much information to share and whether to disclose a long-term relationship whether to actually end it.

He will always deny everything until he makes a choice, inventing the silliest lies to get away with it.

BRING PROOF

 Only after gathering substantial proof may you approach a cheater.

Do not confront him if you don't have "physical" proof, such as naked photos, emails explaining his adoration for her, a jewelry receipt, or a hotel reservation.

If you don't have evidence, you can simply warn him and actually encourage him to be more cautious going forward.

He now has the opportunity to exercise extreme caution, which means you could never discover evidence.

Second, you might be wrong if you lack evidence. He might be loyal to you, and if you falsely accuse him, it could end your relationship.

BE CALM

I'm going to breathe deeply and count to 10 even though I KNOW it's the HARDEST thing to accomplish in this circumstance.

You feel angry, incredibly hurt, and upset all over.

Even when your life is imploding beneath you, you must face him when you are composed.

Don't let your emotions take over; keep your attention on the facts.

If you attack him and yell at him, he'll probably seize the opportunity to storm out of the house, claim he can't talk to you, and correct his narrative.

Make sure you have the necessary evidence before he draws attention to you snooping. You can respond, "Yes, I acknowledge that spying on you was wrong, but the FACT is that I had a good reason to do that - here's the evidence."

He might try to put the entire incident at your feet. The first person to do it won't be him.

It's far simpler than giving him a rationale for his actions. He'll automatically label you as insane, foolish, insecure, infantile, and a maniac. Keep him from doing that. Avoid arguing.

JEDI MENTAL MAGIC

If he continues to reject it and you have "holes" in your proof, try to accept some of the responsibility. It's only a ploy to get him to confess; you don't have to mean it.

Mention the likelihood that you weren't meeting any of his needs, whether they be sexual, emotional, or otherwise.

It will be lot simpler for him to tell you the truth if he is about to admit it. He appreciates that some of the responsibility was taken off of him.

CHAPTER TWO

TALKING ABOUT THE MATTER

The paradox of living through infidelity is that you now have to act as you should have back then.

However, you now need to execute it deliberately, diligently, and regularly. And you have to do it while being under attack from emotions like emotional exhaustion, grief, fear, regret, guilt, and fury.

Today, communication is crucial to success. If you want to save your marriage, discussing adultery with your spouse after cheating has taken place is a requirement.

And it's not enjoyable.

Contrary to popular belief, more marriages than not survive infidelity.

According to relationship experts, men who cheat on their wives are less likely to feel emotionally attached to their affair partners, which increases the likelihood that their marriages will last.

Anyone who has operated a boat understands that one of the most crucial lessons to learn at a young age is how to cross a wake safely. The second leading cause of boater injuries is improper wake crossing, particularly at high speeds.

It takes planning, expertise, and caution to cross over another boat's wake safely. It will feel like hitting a cement wall if you dive headfirst into a strong swell.

However, cutting through at a reduced pace and at an angle, a smooth transition and the capacity to resume speed and position are made possible by speed.

The same is true of communication, and no time is this truer than when you are discussing adultery with your spouse after cheating has taken place.

It makes sense that infidelity leaves a large emotional wake. You can't just assume you have a calm lake to yourself and drive around on it mindlessly.

After adultery has taken place, discussing infidelity with your partner involves more than just the "what." The "what" is surrounded by the "how," "when," "where," and "why."

You're on the rig if you're thinking, "That sounds like any kind of healthy communication," Consider, however, that a UK survey of 5,000 respondents found that Poor communication was the most frequently cited cause of infidelity by both sexes.

And since the offense has already occurred, you're required to communicate a ton. It seems incredibly unlikely, much alone just. However, it is possible to make it so that communication after the affair is preferable to communication before it.

CHAPTER THREE

ADVANCED TRANSPARENCY

If both spouses are dedicated to make the relationship work, there is hope.

The married pair decides they want to work on their marriage after cheating is uncovered and the extramarital relationship is terminated. There's a chance. There is a basis that is shared by both parties. The road ahead can be rough, rocky, and perplexing, but for those who are committed to saving their marriage, the climb will be well worth it in the end. It is not a simple 1-2-3 process for either partner in a relationship to recover from an affair. Both parties in the relationship suffer, but in different ways, and the marriage also suffers. Having complete transparency is a crucial element of rehabilitation.

complete openness within the spheres of support

Couples going through infidelity recovery cannot accomplish this by themselves. The deceived are tempted to band together and share their suffering in order to win sympathy. The betrayer doesn't want the truth to come to light since it's unpleasant, upsetting, and causes additional suffering for others. The transparency must be communicated, though, without actually harming the pair or their support system. A person is forced to make a choice if complete disclosure of the affair is shared with support groups (parents, friends, in-laws, and even children). who or what they support. They form a triangle. And they aren't the ones digesting and sorting things out in therapy. To them, this is unfair. Despite the desire to share being enticing, It's a sensitive conversation to have with the support systems for comfort and support with friends, relatives, and coworkers, it might be uncomfortable and emotionally taxing to have this conversation. However, if you want to transform your marriage into something new, you'll need to take risks. One of those things is complete honesty while still keeping part of the trauma private to the relationship. Perhaps those close to you are aware of the struggle you are going through. Let them know that there is a battle. Simply presenting the facts can be shared without criticizing either party. "We are committed to preserving our union and creating a union like we've never had before. Recently, we've been shaken to the core, but we'll get through it. As we work together to strengthen our marriage to the point where it needs to be, we would appreciate your love and support. You don't have to answer questions or provide personal information, but you should be honest about the fact that things aren't ideal and that you're committed to your future. The assistance of loved ones will be essential in the upcoming trek. Though the couple isn't compelled to work through the affair together—and subsequently still have the criticism, questioning, or unsolicited advice from the triangulated party—by keeping some of the details private, it really helps them recover more quickly.

Complete honesty in the relationship.

Couples must be open with each other.

There can be no unanswered questions. The betrayed deserves to know the information if they need or choose to. Hiding the facts simply increases the risk of a secondary trauma when specifics are later found. These are also challenging talks to have, but a couple needs to be open and honest about the past if they want to move forward. It's crucial for the individual asking the questions to understand that they might not want all the answers and to make a decision about what information they truly want or do not want to know in order to heal.

complete openness in technology

Due to the convenience of meeting new people and hiding unsuitable relationships, relationship problems are made easier in today's world of social media and technology. The devices of each partner in a relationship must be accessible. This does not imply that you utilize it, but it's crucial to take responsibility for understanding passwords, security codes, and the capacity to access texts and emails. This adds accountability to the relationship as well as aiding in the development of trust.

Complete honesty to oneself

Perhaps the toughest to have is this. The betrayer frequently wants to believe that after the affair is over, their life will return to "normal." Wrong. They must understand the reason(s) behind their affair(s). What brought them about? How come they were tempted? What kept them from being devoted? What were they fond of? Being honest with ourselves can be incredibly challenging, but once we do, we can modify our course to make sure we're moving in the right direction.

One of the most challenging aspects of recovery is complete honesty. But with commitment, even when it is simpler to hide, transparency can aid the partnership in moving toward establishing a basis of strength and honesty.

CHAPTER FOUR

Investigating the incident's cause and fostering positivity

The trust that has been built up in a relationship is undermined by infidelity, sometimes to the point where there is no hope of reconciliation, whether it involves sharing a bed with someone who isn't their spouse or forming an inappropriate emotional connection with a work colleague or an online liaison.

A lot of thoughts and feelings go through the hearts and minds of a couple after one of them has been the victim of infidelity, especially the spouse who was cheated on.

Questions such as, "Who was the affair with?" "How long has it been going on for?" "Is it over or were you just caught red-handed?" "Do you love the person you had the affair with?"; "Do you still love me and our family?", and an endless number of other questions.

"Why?" is probably one of the more important questions. There are many other ways to ask this question, such as "Why did you do this?" or "Why did you turn to someone else instead of me to meet your needs?" Asking these questions can be extremely unpleasant, but by doing so the couple can learn more about their relationship and the wandering partner's thoughts by responding to them honestly.

The goal of asking "why" questions and trying to understand what happened is not to justify the conduct, but rather to reveal the marriage's dynamics and offer potential paths for fortifying the union against potential shocks. If you do it right, realizing the reasons behind the breakup of your relationship can be a liberating step toward rebuilding on more secure ground.

The Value of Understanding the Causes of Infidelity and Affairs.

Every pair and every relationship is unique. Infidelity can be caused by a number of complex circumstances, some of which may have been in the relationship for some time. In some circumstances, the way toward the act of infidelity is transient and in no way indicative of a problem in the relationship. The "why" of infidelity should be investigated because it is crucial for both parties.

The partner who had the affair must comprehend what, if anything, they were missing from the marriage and, consequently, what they were hoping to gain from the affair. Being open and honest about one's actions, The pair will be able to identify any connection gaps by determining whether requirements were clearly conveyed, addressed, or neglected. It also reveals one's expectations and what the betrayed partner needs to know about any unmet needs they may have had in the relationship, as well as why the relationship ended and how to maybe go on. It's also a chance to consider whether they want to fill that need and how they can go about doing so.

To put it another way, understanding what transpired and why it did allow the couple to understand the challenges at hand and map out a route for the future together, with more open lines of communication and a solid foundation. or, if they so choose to separate.

What are some typical motives for having relations in light of this?

The Most Common Motives for Infidelity

There could be one or several causes for a partner to be unfaithful in any given circumstance. Some of these issues are more long-term and take longer to manifest than others; some are less so. These issues can easily be made worse by the availability of opportunities to cheat, especially in our anonymous online age.

Ineffective communication

Communication breakdown is one factor in infidelity. A healthy relationship depends on the couple's ability to communicate effectively. They communicate their needs and worries to each other. When communication goes down, it impacts the relationship's different aspects.

For a number of reasons, including not feeling heard, appreciated, valuable, or safe in the relationship, communication might break down. All of these factors may prevent the couple from being in a position to hear, comprehend, and satisfy one another's needs. An affair is a simple way for a couple to vent their irritation if they are having issues but lack the ability to effectively discuss their concerns and find a solution.

Lack of affection

Warm feelings between a couple should serve to smooth over any potential conflicts and keep the couple involved in their union. It's crucial to feel adored, desired, and valued needs in the partnership that should be satisfied. Sometimes the ignored spouse looks for their needs to be addressed elsewhere because the other spouse lacks the skillset to effectively convey them.

Numerous factors can contribute to a relationship's lack of physical closeness. Accidents can prevent someone from engaging in sexual activity. The libido may be decreased by taking specific drugs or dealing with mental health issues like depression. The desire for sexual closeness and physical intimacy in general does not vanish or disappear for either partner when a couple stops having sex.

A disappointed partner can turn to porn or find another person to have sex with. Due to the accessibility of online hookups and escorts, sexual frustration is common is much easier to handle by looking outside the marriage.

Emotional connection is lost

An alliance can deteriorate with time. It's simple for a couple to lose one another in the shuffle as we become immersed in our lives -- work, kids, making mortgage and other payments without checking in with one another, it's simple for the couple to live beside one another rather than with one another since their goals and identities alter. When an emotional connection is gone, a space is left for another person, such a coworker, to step in and provide support.

Other Motives for Cheating

The factors mentioned above are typically the causes of affairs. People in fulfilling relationships can still be found in some situations unfaithful, and this isn't because their relationship isn't strong enough.

It is understandable that this would be puzzling because our common concept of infidelity is that it stems from a deficiency or a gap in the primary relationship. Infidelity can sometimes happen for other reasons. These may consist of:

The allure and allurement of transgression: Stepping over boundaries to get forbidden food. This is mentioned in the Proverbs when it discusses adultery. We believe the myth that the forbidden fruit is, in some way, tastier and more rewarding than what is given to us.

Self exploration

Self-exploration might be appealing to someone who wants to learn more about themselves, especially emotions they have never felt or experienced to want to have an affair. The routines of life, including a couple's sex lives, may bring one partner to have an affair to experience something different.

The draw of a life not lived: For those that married young and felt like they never lived their own life, or for those who are getting older, the life not lived becomes an attractive option. Wistfulness and the desire to do things one did not do before, or to reconnect with an old flame to explore what might have been, can lead someone down the path of infidelity. With social media platforms, finding and contacting those old flames has never been easier, and many affairs are born of this.

These other reasons, including psychological issues such as sex addiction, personality disorders or childhood trauma may have a hand in why one partner cheats. Knowing these reasons does not excuse bad behavior, but it certainly illuminates it. The pain of being cheated on does not go away just because there is an explanation for it, but it is better to have information than not. Knowing these reasons does not excuse bad behavior, but it certainly illuminates it. Personality disorders, sex addiction, or childhood trauma may play a role in why one partner cheats.

CHAPTER FIVE

Developing trust and controlling sensitivities

Infidelity victims may experience an emotional roller coaster. The majority of couples who are involved in the tragedy of an affair say that they have never experienced such strong emotions.

For example, a lot of betrayed partners obsess over the affair and wonder, "How could my partner do this to me?" I can never again have faith in them.

The straying partner, on the other hand, frequently claims, "I used to beg my partner for more attention and I get it from my lover. No matter what I do to earn my spouse's trust, I'm not confident that she will ever do so.

RELEARNING TO TRUST

After a betrayal, rebuilding trust is a difficult and gradual process. Nevertheless, there are circumstances where there is cause for optimism. To begin healing from the pain, both couples must first acknowledge that they each have work to do.

 The actions of your spouse matter more than the words they use.

The unfaithful partner must: Be truthful, disclose the affair fully, and find a means to make amends or show regret.

After the finding, deal with the traumatic emotions, and be willing to answer inquiries. It must come to an end.

Be prepared to really apologize for cheating and swear not to do it again.

Additionally, if you are the one who betrayed your relationship, you need to concentrate on being transparent and winning back their trust. This could take the form of daily check-ins or assuring them that you love them and won't cheat on them again. I'd hate to see you go.

If you have betrayed someone, consider what you may do to win back your partner's trust. This can entail making frequent excuses or outlining the betrayal in detail. Most importantly, you need to show empathy by using phrases like "I get it. I can see how you might experience this. I would struggle too if I were in your shoes.

The betrayed partner must: Remember to treat yourself with kindness, especially when you're having a difficult day and thinking about your partner's infidelity.

You should also express your emotions to your partner, but refrain from making accusations.

Keep the events leading up to the affair from being repeated. Talking about it endlessly could make the wounds worse.

Find a method to accept your partner's behavior or at least, to forgive them, and endeavor to do so.

FINAL WORK FOR BOTH PARTNERS

Discussing emotional emotions with one other in a respectful manner free of blame, judgment and criticism is necessary.

Either the partners can find a way to connect sexually and emotionally, or they risk becoming more physically intimate.

Additionally, they must improve their communication and spend more time together. This includes social habits like taking daily walks or eating meals together.

How to handle your triggers.

It is up to you to manage and overcome your triggers. It is not your partner's responsibility to pay closer attention, be more considerate, open, cheerful, peaceful, etc. so you won't get provoked.

To prevent your current relationship from being impacted by past injuries, work through them.

Become conscious of your reactions and the narrative you construct about your spouse in your thoughts. Own it as something you created. Whichever element of it is true can be acknowledged by your lover.

Recognize how to assist the hurt child. The one who is there for them is you, not anyone else not going to leave them behind. In time, they will be able to depend on your presence and self-love.

Take a break from communication to address your triggers to prevent them from becoming more intense.

Avoid using the words "always" and "never" in your reasoning. Feelings that are triggered often become generalized.

Before you draw any judgments, take the time to investigate what is going on with your spouse, what led them to act that way, what drove them, and ask questions. Learn about them and accept their truth.

CHAPTER SIX

HEALING AND FORGIVENESS

After being cheated on, you could continue to struggle with self-doubt and concerns of trust. Even if you decide to give your partner another chance, building trust may take a lot of time to accomplish.

Below are some techniques that can assist you in taking the first steps toward recovery;

Accept instead of avoiding

You must frequently first come to grips with what happened in order to heal.

No matter how hard you try to forget what happened, you can find yourself revisiting those memories when you're doing other things.

A trauma like this may make leaning into it too painful to even consider. But once you acknowledge it, you can start looking into the causes, which might help the healing process.

You can start accepting underlying relationship concerns, including a lack of intimacy or communication, and look into solutions rather than being caught in a never-ending loop of self-doubt and self-criticism.

Practice embracing challenging feelings

After a betrayal, unpleasant feelings may surface. You can feel sick or heartbroken, embarrassed, angry, or spiteful.

Of course, you can try to escape this discomfort by trying to ignore or block what occurred.

Although suppressing or masking uncomfortable emotions may seem safe and easy, doing so can make it harder to control them.

You can deal with certain emotions more well if you give them names, such as wrath, regret, or grief.

Sitting with your emotions can be easier and less terrifying if you can identify them. A greater understanding of your emotions can then guide you in developing effective coping mechanisms.

Obtain assistance from others

It's not always simple to talk openly about betrayal. You might not want to discuss it. A person who has violated your confidence may also make it difficult for you to confide in others. However, humans require emotional support, particularly when they are under pressure. Although they may not need to be aware of every detail, your loved ones can still provide distractions when necessary and company when you don't want to be by yourself.

It's acceptable to ask your pals for advice and to communicate your feelings in a respectful manner.

You might want to tread lightly when bringing up a partner's infidelity while with friends. Save the information for your closest loved ones because gossip can make a terrible situation more worse.

Think about what you need.

As you start to come to terms with the trauma's shock, pay close attention to your needs:

Try a warm bath, or calming music to relax and improve your sleep instead of staying awake and thinking about it.

Favorite movies and TV series might offer solace and peace, but try to incorporate some other pastimes as well like exercise, reading, etc are all beneficial for elevating mood. It is also advisable that you go for therapy and counselling.

Conclusion

Understanding the reasons for the infidelity helps the couple make sense of what happened and, perhaps, learn how to avoid it in the future. There could have been some unmet needs. It is impossible to expect people to fulfill wants that are not voiced because they are unable to read minds.

The other spouse may have indicated additional needs, but for one reason or another, they cannot be met. The couple must come up with a solution that benefits them both. Marriage requires a couple to confront problems head-on rather than avoiding them and turning to infidelity for solace.

Commitment and open communication are essential to maintaining a relationship, and infidelity does not spell the end of a partnership. A couple that has experienced infidelity may be able to work through the underlying problems and come out on the other side stronger than ever.

57